THE PÈRE MARQUETTE
LECTURE IN THEOLOGY
1999

MORAL THEOLOGY AT THE
END OF THE CENTURY

CHARLES E. CURRAN

Elizabeth Scurlock University Professor of Human Values
Southern Methodist University

MARQUETTE
UNIVERSITY

PRESS

Library of Congress Cataloguing-in-Publication Data

Curran, Charles E.
  Moral theology at the end of the century / by Charles E.
Curran.
  p. cm. — (The Père Marquette lecture in theology ; 1999)
  Includes bibliographical references.
  ISBN 0-87462-579-3
  1. Christian ethics—Catholic authors. 2. Catholic
Church—Doctrines—History—20th century. I. Title. II. Series.
  BJ1249 .C819 1999
  241'.042'0904—dc21   99-6135

COPYRIGHT © 1999
MARQUETTE UNIVERSITY PRESS
MILWAUKEE WI 53201-1881

Manufactured in the United States of America

Member, ASSOCIATION OF AMERICAN UNIVERSITY PRESSES

MARQUETTE UNIVERSITY PRESS
MILWAUKEE

The Association of Jesuit University Presses

Foreword

This year's Père Marquette Lecture in Theology marks the thirtieth lecture in the series, inaugurated in 1969 to commemorate the missions and explorations of Père Jacques Marquette, S.J. (1637-75). Held annually under the auspices of Marquette University's Department of Theology, it continues to be funded generously by the Joseph A. Auchter Family Endowment Fund, named after Milwaukee-native Joseph A. Auchter (1894-1986), a banker, paper-industry executive, and long-time supporter of education. The fund was established by his children as a memorial to their father.

Charles E. Curran

For close to forty years Charles E. Curran has played a pivotal role in the teaching, mediation, and development of Roman Catholic moral theology, both in North America, throughout the Catholic Church, and, increasingly, among Christian ethicists of differing traditions. His accomplishments within moral theology appear similarly boundless, for his teaching and writing covers the areas of fundamental moral theology, social, economic, historical, medical and sexual moral theology. And he has been a key participant in the important discussions about academic freedom in the ecclesiastical context, particularly in the American university setting.

Born in March of 1934, Fr. Curran was ordained as a priest in the Roman Catholic diocese of Rochester, New York. Although he expected to work in parish-ministry, after the completion of his seminary education at St. Bernard's College in 1955, his bishop sent him to Rome for further studies, which he undertook both at the Pontifical Gregorian University and Academia Alfonsiana, where he earned a Doctorate in Sacred Theology from each institution in 1961. That year Fr. Curran returned to teach at the seminary where he had studied. He has taught moral theology ever since: St. Bernard's Seminary (1961-65), The Catholic University of America (1965-89), visiting professorships at Cornell University (1987-88), University of Southern California (1988-90), Auburn University, Alabama (1990-91). Since 1991 he has been the Elizabeth Scurlock University Professor of Human Values at Southern Methodist University, in Dallas, Texas. He is past president of the Catholic Theological Society of America (1969-70), the Society for Christian Ethics (1971-72), and the American Theological Society (1989-90), and serves on the editorial boards of several theological journals (*Église et théologie, Horizons, Journal of Religious Ethics, Annual of Society of Christian Ethics*).

Since 1966 he has regularly published books and collections of his essays through Fides Publishers—then, later, the University of Notre Dame Press—on major aspects of contemporary moral theology. These include: *Christian Morality Today* (1966), *Ongoing Revision: Studies in Moral Theology* (1975), *Issues in*

Sexual and Medical Ethics (1978), *Directions in Catholic Social Ethics* (1985), *The Living Tradition of Catholic Moral Theology* (1992). 1986 saw the publication of his important *Faithful Dissent* (Kansas City, MO: Sheed and Ward), and in recent years he has published on the history of moral theology (*History and Contemporary Issues: Studies in Moral Theology* [New York: Continuum, 1996], and *The origins of Moral Theology in the United States: Three Different Approaches* [Washington: Georgetown University Press, 1997]). The present year sees the publication of his co-authored work, *The Catholic Moral Tradition Today: A Synthesis* (Washington: Georgetown University Press, 1999).

Among his many editorial contributions is the Paulist Press series, *Readings in Moral Theology*, begun in 1979 with his long-time colleague, Richard A. McCormick, S.J. Topics in this series have covered timely areas of contemporary moral theology, ranging from moral norms (1979) to the use of Scripture in moral theology (1984) to natural law (1991) and to Pope John Paul II's relationship to contemporary moral theology (1998).

He has been honored in the *New York Times*, by ABC News, by the Catholic Theological Society of America with the John Courtney Murray award (1972), and by the University of Charleston, West Virginia, and Concordia College, Oregon, with honorary doctorates.

In this thirtieth Père Marquette Lecture in Theology Fr. Curran brings to bear his wide learning and experience to speak on "Moral Theology at the End of the Century," where he addresses the past, present, and possible future for Roman Catholic moral theology in the coming century, the third millennium.

Mark F. Johnson
27 March 1999

MORAL THEOLOGY AT THE END OF THE CENTURY

The title of this lecture makes no claim to originality. The title comes from an influential article written by Thomas J. Bouquillon in 1899—"Moral Theology at the End of the Nineteenth Century."[1] In that article Bouquillon, the first holder of the Chair of Moral Theology at The Catholic University of America, deals with the deficiencies of moral theology at the time and makes suggestions for the renewal of moral theology.

At the end of the twentieth century as a moral theologian in the United States, I welcome the opportunity to use the prestigious Père Marquette Lecture to address the analogous topic of moral theology at the end of the twentieth century. Like Bouquillon's article, this lecture must find some way to narrow so huge a topic.

The most outstanding characteristic of Catholic moral theology in the United States in the twentieth century has been the dramatic changes that have occurred. The distance between the discussion among priest professors at the end of the last century about

---

This lecture is dedicated to the memory of two moral theologians:
  Thomas G. Dailey (1928-1998)
  Bernhard Häring (1912-1998)

the manuals of moral theology with the aim of training confessors for the sacrament of penance and debates about feminist ethics in Catholic moral theology well illustrate these startling developments. James M. Gustafson, the eminent Protestant ethicist who has been an insightful and sympathetic critic of Catholic moral theology, refers to the "intellectual leap or gulf" between these different genres of moral theology. Gustafson points out that the story behind this change is "so dense and complex that perhaps no one can competently tell it at the present time."[2]

With Gustafson's caveat in mind, this essay will attempt to give some understanding of what has occurred in Catholic moral theology without pretending to be the last word on the subject. The purpose of this lecture is to try to explain, analyze, and understand how these developments took place. Catholic moral theology, like all theological disciplines, serves three publics—the church, the academy, and the broader society. This study will use these three different aspects of the discipline to analyze how the dramatic changes have occurred. The primary context for moral theology is ecclesial, since moral theology reflects in a systematic and scientific way on the moral life of the members of the community of the church. The first and longest section will analyze the ecclesial aspect of the discipline. The second section will discuss the academic aspects of moral theology in the United States. Catholic moral theology has always given an important place to human reason, and theology had a very central role in the origins of universities under the auspices of the church. The third section will consider the societal aspects that have influenced the development of moral theology. Since moral theology is concerned not only about life in the church, but above all about life in the world, these societal changes are bound to affect the discipline. A fourth and final section will point out the continuities in Catholic moral theology despite these startling changes.

I. ECCLESIAL CONTEXT

The changes that have occurred in Catholic moral theology in this century have come about especially since the Second Vatican Council (1962-1965). There was little or no change or creative development in moral theology for the first sixty years of this century. The manuals of moral theology with their primary purpose of training confessors for their role as judges in the sacrament of penance continued to be identified with all of moral theology. The legal model of the manuals saw law as the objective norm of morality and conscience as the subjective norm with specific moral actions often considered in the light of the Ten Commandments. The primary concern was to establish what acts are sinful and whether or not they constitute mortal or venial sin. Human reason, especially in the form of the natural law, was the primary source for moral theology with Scripture playing a very subordinate role often used merely as a proof text. However, the teaching of the hierarchical magisterium, especially the pope, and the opinions of theologians on disputed questions played an ever greater role in determining the morality of particular acts.[3]

Pre-Vatican II

The fact that the moral theology of the manuals remained *the* Catholic approach to moral theology until the beginning of Vatican II is somewhat surprising in light of the ferment and creativity that had come to the fore at the end of the nineteenth century.

In his essay written in 1899, Thomas Bouquillon, a figure of worldwide repute in Catholic moral theology, severely castigated the manuals in the light of the *Summa* of Thomas Aquinas. Bouquillon insisted on the need for moral theology to employ more theological aspects and to recognize the importance of the speculative and systematic nature of the discipline in addition to its practical concerns. In keeping with the directives of Pope Leo XIII, Bouquillon urged the use of the neoscholastic method based on Thomas Aquinas.[4] Bouquillon was not alone. The influential seminary rector, John B. Hogan, in his 1898 book *Clerical Studies*, rejected neoscholasticism, insisted on the need for a more inductive approach, recognized errors in past Catholic teaching, and pleaded for the recognition of more gray areas in moral theology. He objected especially to the manuals' understanding of mortal and venial sin, even disagreeing in theory with the very distinction itself, and pointing out that in practice one could never judge the person only on the basis of the external act. The outsider can never know the subjective disposition and moral reality of the person who has acted.[5] Such an understanding basically pulls the rug out from underneath the whole purpose of the manuals. Hogan was even stronger than Bouquillon in his criticism of the manuals.

In an earlier 1896 book, John Talbot Smith made an even more biting indictment of moral theology strongly objecting to the fact that "moral theology is the chief study of our seminaries, holding the first place in the curriculum and in the mind of the student." Many believe that moral theology should not only be dethroned but also reformed and renovated; the very appealing and practical goal of moral theology has distorted the whole seminary curriculum." Smith ranked the importance of the disciplines for the formation of the priest in the seminary in this order—1) Scripture, 2) philosophy, 3) dogmatic theology, 4) general literature, 5) a reformed moral theology.[6]

However, nothing really changed until Vatican II as the manuals remained the textbooks for moral theology in seminaries. Moral theology was either equal to, or slightly less than, dogmatic theology in terms of the number of hours reserved for the subject.[7] Occasional criticisms continued, but moral theology remained a practical discipline dealing primarily with sins and had very little of the scientific or theological about it.[8]

What explains these facts? The Catholic Church in the twentieth century became more defensive, authoritarian, and centralized than it had ever been before. The condemnations of Americanism (1899) and Modernism (1907) and the responses of the Biblical Commission at that time rejecting any use of historical criticism in biblical interpretation put a damper on intellectual stimulation and creativity in the Catholic community. Before Modernism there was some creativity even in the immigrant Catholicism of the United States as illustrated not only by the criticisms of moral theology at the end of the century but also by the articles on Scripture and dogmatic theology in the *New York Review* which was published in Dunwoodie, the seminary of the Archdiocese of New York, from 1905 to 1908. The condemnation of Modernism with the subsequent oath against Modernism to be taken by church officials, those who receive church academic degrees, and professors in seminaries, as well as the establishment of vigilance committees in every diocese, created an atmosphere that stifled any intellectual curiosity and creativity. Mere repetition of what had previously been said characterized American Catholic theology in general until Vatican II and played an important role in the continued use of the manuals of moral theology.[9]

In keeping with their fear of dialogue with modern thought, the twentieth century popes continued and strengthened the late nineteenth century insistence of Pope Leo XIII that Catholic theology had to be taught according to the method, the principles, and the teaching of Thomas Aquinas.[10] This legislation coming from Rome insured that neoscholasticism reigned supreme in Catholic intellectual life and no modern approaches were accepted. The manuals in both dogmatic and moral theology were seen to be in line with this neoscholastic approach. However, in reality the manuals of moral theology were not Thomistic as Thomas Bouquillon pointed out explicitly and correctly in 1899.[11]

How did it come about that in reality the manuals of moral theology continued in existence and were thought to be an illustration of the use of neoscholasticism? Just as church authorities had sanctioned the work of Thomas Aquinas, so too church authorities promoted the work of Alphonsus Ligouri who was canonized a saint in 1839, made a doctor of the church in 1871, and declared the patron of confessors and moral theologians in 1950.[12] Undoubtedly the prudential approach that Alphonsus showed in dealing with particular moral issues deserved commendation. However, his strong support of papal authority, his promotion of Marian piety, and the ultramontanism of many of his followers also contributed to his recognition by papal authority in the nineteenth and twentieth century.[13] Papal promotion of Alphonsus Ligouri, whose approach was identified with the manuals, thus insured, especially in the conditions of the early twentieth century, that the manuals of moral theology would continue in existence. It is true that the manuals of moral theology and Alphonsus himself quoted Thomas Aquinas more than any other theologian. However, the manuals of moral theology did not follow the method and approach of Thomas Aquinas but used a legalistic model concentrating on the sinfulness of acts rather than a teleological model based on the virtues of the person.

Despite the anti-intellectual climate, the fear of theological innovation, and the tendency merely to quote those who had gone before, there were some sparks of creativity, but they remained comparatively few and far between. John A. Ryan (1869-1945), a former student of, and later successor to, Bouquillon at Catholic University, whose major contribution was in the area of social ethics, rejected the perverted faculty argument as a proof for the immorality of artificial contraception. The perverted faculty argument maintained that artificial contraception was wrong because it went against the God-given procreative purpose of the sexual faculty. Ryan argued on the basis of the analogous case that the ultimate malice of lying was not in the perversion of the nature and purpose of the faculty but rather in the violation of the neighbor's right to truth. Ryan, in keeping with a longtime concern of his, made the argument against contraception on the basis on its consequences.[14] In his social ethics Ryan had often appealed to consequences and the principle of expediency—the identification of morality and expediency. Such an approach allowed him to show how the morally good action would also be beneficial for all concerned. Good ethics is good economics. However, Ryan never theoretically explained or explored his principle of expediency.[15] After rejecting the perverted faculty argument in the *American Ecclesiastical Review* in 1929, Ryan at the request of the editor added a section to show that the church condemned artificial contraception.[16] The editor obviously did not want to give the impression that the Catholic teaching on artificial contraception was wrong or should change.

Other indications of some creativity occasionally surfaced. For example, a Redemptorist priest, Francis Connell, who taught moral theology at The Catholic University of America from 1940 to 1958, recognized with regard to the object of the moral act some of the problems contemporary revisionist moral theologians have proposed in their unwillingness to define the moral object in terms of the physical aspect of the object. Connell insisted that the proper understanding of the object of the act had to include the first moral circumstance—e.g., murder is the moral object, not killing. He also applied this to lying but not to any controversial issues such as artificial contraception.[17] Gerald Kelly, the professor of moral theology at the Jesuit Scholasticate in St. Mary's, Kansas, from 1937 to 1963, in his first published article argued in favor of the morality of artificial insemination with the husband's semen if the semen were obtained by moral means and not by masturbation,[18] but he quickly accepted the condemnation of such artificial insemination by Pope Pius XII in 1949.[19] Thus in general the manuals remained the Catholic way of approaching moral theology and there was comparatively little creativity or theological initiative. The primary concern in the literature was a casuistical approach to particular issues including some newer questions raised especially by medical technology.

As the twentieth century progressed with a greater role given in Catholic teaching and life to the papal teaching office, it was only natural that papal teaching assumed an ever greater importance in moral theology. Ever since the nineteenth century the papal teaching office, including the Roman congregations such as the Holy Office (now known as the Congregation for the Doctrine of the Faith), have been giving responses to particular dilemmas and questions about such issues as abortion and ectopic pregnancy.[20]

Aloysius Sabetti (1839-1898), in his manual which later became the most widely used moral manual published by someone teaching in the United States,[21] did not have a special section on the hierarchical magisterium.[22] Sabetti's very comprehensive index has no listing for magisterium or the sources of theology. The four entries under "Pope" deal with issues of canon law. The manual obviously relied on papal teaching and the responses of the Roman congregations where they were applicable, but there was no separate discussion of the role and function of the hierarchical magisterium. The growing role of the papal magisterium is illustrated in the many addresses of Pope Pius XII (1939-1958) on medical moral issues. Gerald Kelly, in his *Medico—Moral Problems* (1958), refers to the teaching of Pius XII on twenty-two specific issues.[23]

Since 1941, the Jesuits John C. Ford and Gerald A. Kelly had been writing commentaries on contemporary moral theology for *Theological Studies*. They decided to put together in a more permanent book form related topics dealing with aspects of moral theology. Two volumes were eventually published— *Contemporary Moral Theology,* vol. 1, *Questions in Fundamental Moral Theology* and vol. 2, *Marriage*

Questions.[24] The first three chapters in the first volume deal with the hierarchical magisterium. Papal teaching also plays a major role in the second volume. Edwin Lisson, in his analysis of Kelly's sources of moral theology, treats the magisterium first and describes it as "the foundation of moral theology."[25] Thus the hierarchical magisterium's role in moral theology was recognized as most important and explicitly treated as such.

What is the binding force of such papal teaching according to Ford and Kelly? The two Jesuit moral theologians developed their approach in the light of the 1950 encyclical of Pius XII *Humani generis.* In that document the pope referred to the hierarchical magisterium as the proximate and universal norm of truth for theologians, applied to the ordinary noninfallible papal magisterium the words of Jesus from Luke 10:16 "He who hears you, hears me," and concluded that whenever the pope goes out of his way to speak on a disputed point, it is no longer a matter for free debate among theologians.[26] While recognizing that *Humani generis* was primarily discussing papal encyclicals, Ford and Kelly give the same authority to other papal teachings such as the addresses given by the pope to different medical groups. Gerald Kelly's change on artificial insemination well illustrates the response that theologians must give to such papal teaching. In fairness, Ford and Kelly are not literalists or fundamentalists—the papal documents require some interpretation. It must be clear that the pope intends to decisively settle the controverted issue in these particular talks or documents. However, once the pope takes such a stand on a disputed issue, theologians can no longer disagree.[27]

By the late 1950s and the early 1960s the issue of artificial contraception for spouses became most prominent. Protestants and most people in society no longer accepted the immorality of such actions. However, no Catholic moral theologian publicly questioned the official hierarchical teaching until 1963. The dispute before that time was between Catholics and others. Non-Catholics did not accept the natural law or rational arguments supporting the ban on artificial contraception. The Catholic insistence that its teaching was based on human reason or natural law and its insistence on authoritative papal teaching were in some tension. The tension would become even more pronounced after 1963 when some Catholic moral theologians questioned the papal teaching. In the light of this, Ford and Kelly recognized some difficulties in all people accepting as conclusive the natural law argument against artificial contraception and relied more on the authoritative teaching of the church, which in their judgment was irrevocable with regard to contraception.[28] The later Ford insisted on the infallible character of this teaching based on the ordinary infallible teaching of all the bishops throughout the world and down through the ages together with the pope.[29] As the twentieth century progressed the primary and decisive role of papal teaching is evident in Catholic moral theology.

There can be no doubt that Catholic moral theology in the first six decades of the twentieth century can be described as papalist, but some nuances are in order. The role of the papal magisterium and its decisive importance grew as the century developed and was especially evident in sexual and medical ethics. Writing in 1969 in the post-Vatican II era, Francis Broderick, the sympathetic biographer of John A. Ryan, refers to the progressive social thinker who advocated many of the New Deal reforms long before Franklin Delano Roosevelt as a papalist. Broderick, reflecting on Ryan's work six years after his biography of Ryan, maintains that papalist is a more accurate description of Ryan than liberal or reformer.[30] In his earlier biography, he tended to use those descriptions.[31] I disagree somewhat. No Catholic theologian even in the early part of the twentieth century was ever going to disagree with papal teaching. Broderick correctly points out that Ryan changed his position on sterilization of the mentally ill after Pius XI's condemnation of sterilization in *Casti connubii* in 1930. Ryan also defended Leo XIII's position on church and state which caused great embarrassment to many American Catholics; he pushed for industry-wide councils only after Pius XI's encyclical *Quadragesimo anno* calling for such changes. But in his earlier and more systematic works, Ryan gave scarce attention to papal teaching. One is amazed at the very few references to papal teaching in *A Living Wage* (1906) and *Distributive Justice* (1916).[32] Ryan's arguments were based primarily and almost exclusively on human reason in dealing with economics and the issues of the time. Ryan's supporters saw the 1931 encyclical as proof of Ryan's Catholic orthodoxy. Without doubt, he makes more direct appeals to *Quadragesimo anno*

(1931) than he had earlier to *Rerum novarum* (1891), but he often does it to wrap himself in the papal mantle.[33]

Successors of Ryan gave much more importance to papal teaching. John F. Cronin, in the preface to his *Social Principles and Economic Life*, acknowledges in his preface that "the primary sources used are the social writings and addresses of recent popes."[34] Each chapter begins with long citations from different papal documents.

Cronin later recognized the very fundamentalistic hermeneutic used by himself and other Catholic scholars in interpreting papal teaching. It never occurred to him in the pre-Vatican II period that these documents were historically and culturally conditioned and limited by their Italian and Germanic mind sets. Form criticism was unknown to scholars like Cronin. "Probably we would not have dared to use it on documents of the magisterium, even had we known what it meant."[35]

Before Vatican II Catholic moral theology was identified with the manuals with their limited scope of determining sinfulness and degrees of sinfulness, a legal model with law as the remote and objective norm of morality, no real use of Scripture, a recognition of the role of human reason and natural law, and a predominant and growing emphasis on authoritative hierarchical teaching.

Vatican II

The most significant ecclesial reality that deeply affected moral theology and the whole life of the Catholic Church was the Second Vatican Council (1962-65). At the very least, it is necessary to dispute the commonly accepted notion that Vatican II appeared out of nowhere and dramatically changed the life of the Catholic Church by moving from the top down. The danger exists of seeing the renewal as another instance of the primacy and seemingly independent role of church authority. Yes, the Vatican Council did come from higher authority in the church and did bring about most significant changes. But in reality these changes came originally from the grass roots. There never would have been a Vatican II if it were not for the biblical, liturgical, catechetical, and lay movements that had been growing in the worldwide Catholic community. This is certainly true in the area of moral theology as well. Ever since the eighteenth century the Tübingen School had been criticizing the manuals of moral theology even though this criticism did not have that much effect. In 1954 Bernard Häring published in German his important *Law of Christ* whose very subtitle indicated its move away from the manuals—*A Moral Theology for Priests and Laity.*[36] Häring's approach was more biblical, personalistic, and theological and set the tone for much of the subsequent renewal in moral theology during and after Vatican II. Thanks to the writings of Ford and Kelly Americans were aware of the work of Häring and other attempts to reform moral theology, e.g., Fritz Tillmann, Emile

Mersch, and Gérard Gilleman. Ford and Kelly appreciated some aspects in the new approaches but insisted on the need for manuals and pointed out the dangers involved in the new approaches.[37] Thus, even English speakers in the United States were aware of a growing criticism of the manuals of moral theology and the calls for renewal which were later associated with Vatican II.

What were the significant developments of Vatican II that affected moral theology? Since the contemporary period is comparatively well known, this section will briefly summarize five very important aspects of Vatican II that have influenced the development of moral theology. First, the twofold methodological approach to reform and renewal at Vatican II involved bringing the church up to date through a dialogue with the contemporary world and going back to the sources of Scripture, tradition, and the patristic period. This two-pronged approach to renewal and reform avoids the extreme dangers of a simple return to the past or a simple acceptance of all that is happening in contemporary society. After the council, however, it has become clear that the two different approaches exist in some tension with one another. Advocates of bringing the church up to date have continued to push for more reform in the church, whereas the proponents of going back to the sources have been fearful of further changes.[38]

Second, many Catholic theologians agree with Bernard Lonergan that the most fundamental change at Vatican II involved adopting a historically conscious methodology in place of the classicism which reigned before. Historical consciousness gives more importance to the particular, the individual, and the contingent; whereas classicism insists on the eternal, the immutable, and the unchanging. While recognizing the need for both continuity and discontinuity, historical consciousness opposes sheer existentialism that sees the present with no connection to the past or future and no relationship to present realities and persons. A more historically conscious methodology is more inductive than a classicist approach which dominated Catholic theology in the pre-Vatican II period.[39]

Third, Vatican II emphasized the person and the primacy of the person. The first chapter in the Pastoral Constitution on the Church in the Modern World is entitled "The Dignity of the Human Person."[40] The historic Declaration on Religious Liberty changed the older teaching denying religious liberty by grounding its teaching in the dignity of the human person.[41]

Fourth, Vatican II opened the door to ecumenical dialogue. The non-Catholic observers at the Council played a significant role outside the formal sessions of the meeting and were generally very positive about their experience.[42] The Constitution on the Church and the Decree on Ecumenism encouraged ecumenical dialogue and contact. From that time forward, Catholic theologians have worked ecumenically and dialogued with non-Catholic authors and positions in doing their theology.

Fifth, Vatican II also called for some changes that were more specifically aimed at moral theology. The Decree on the Training of Priests succinctly pointed out a general direction for the reform of moral

theology. "Special care should be given to the per-
fecting of moral theology. Its scientific presentation
should draw more fully on the teaching of holy
Scripture and should throw light upon the exalted
vocation of the faithful in Christ and their obliga-
tion to bring forth fruit and charity for the life of the
world."[43] This concise observation brings three important aspects to the fore—the importance of Scripture for Catholic theology and life; the call of all
Christians to holiness as found in the Constitution
on the Church; and the insistence of the Pastoral
Constitution on the Church in the Modern World
that Christians and the church must work together
with all people of good will to bring about justice
and peace in our world. Intrinsically connected with
the greater role of Scripture was the recognition that
faith and grace must penetrate and influence what-
ever the Christian does. The Pastoral Constitution
on the Church in the Modern World pointed out:
"One of the gravest errors of our time is the di-
chotomy between the faith that many profess and
the practice of their daily lives."[44]

These developments at Vatican II had a profound
impact on moral theology. The following paragraphs will summarize the most important aspects.[45]
First, the manuals of moral theology ceased to exist.
The scope of moral theology had to be much broader
than simply defining what is sinful and the degrees
of sinfulness. In addition in the light of the emphasis
on the person, theologians pointed out that sin
cannot be adequately understood on the basis of the
objective act alone. The external act can and should
be described as right or wrong, but the presence of

sin and its degree depends on the subjective involvement of the person. The dramatic falling off in the
number of Catholics "going to confession" confirms
this understanding.

Second, the emphasis on the role of Scripture and
grace and the importance of the person have changed
the primary focus of moral theology from the act to
the person, from doing to being. The biblical con-
cepts of conversion, loving response to God's gra-
cious gift, and change of heart have come to the fore.
The person's fundamental response to God's loving
gift determines the basic reality of who the person is.
This basic orientation of the person involves living
out the baptismal commitment to love God above
all things and to love one's neighbor as oneself. This
basic orientation or fundamental option has been
developed in different ways depending on anthropological and philosophical considerations.

The emphasis on the person as subject and agent
has called for the renewed recognition of the importance of the virtues in the Christian life. Virtues both
make the person the type of person she is and
influence how the person will act. The scriptural
narrative and story are very important in shaping the
person and the virtues of the person. Thus narrative
theology has a significant role to play in moral
theology.

Third, the Vatican II effort to relate faith, grace,
and Scripture more clearly to daily life both gave a
new understanding to Christian life in the world and
raised new methodological issues. Christology and
soteriology now have great import for the life of
Christians in the world. Above all eschatology came

to the fore. What is the proper relationship between the fullness of the reign of God and what is happening here and now? The newer emphasis also raised the question about the proper role and function of the Scriptures in moral theology. Likewise the debated issue of what is unique and distinctive about Christian morality came to the fore. The manuals of moral theology with their natural law approach had assumed that the morality proposed for Christians was exactly the same as the morality proposed for all human beings because it was based on the same human nature. Now, with a greater emphasis on grace, faith, and Christology, the question naturally arose about what is distinctive or unique about Christian morality. Does this uniqueness affect the intentionality and motivation alone or does it also have some effect on the content?

Liberation theology, which arose in Latin America after the council, built on this newer approach. The Gospel message of liberation applies also to the social, political, economic, and cultural levels of human existence. The Scriptures also heavily emphasize God's special concern for the poor and the needy. One can thus see how liberation theology grew out of the developments at Vatican II to overcome the split between faith and daily life.

Fourth, as a result of Vatican II's criticism of neoscholasticism and emphasis on dialogue, there no longer existed *the* Catholic philosophy. Despite the importance of grace, faith, and Scripture, the traditional Catholic emphasis on the human and human reason continued. Theology needs to employ philosophical and anthropological understandings in order to study faith and life in a systematic and scientific way. Different theologies have adopted different philosophical approaches. Historical consciousness and the turn to the person as subject and agent have influenced the philosophical approaches used in Catholic moral theology. Even in the Pastoral Constitution on the Church in the Modern World, one sees both a greater personalism and a greater historical consciousness as exemplified in the importance given to the signs of the time and the more inductive methodology. Liberation theologies in all their forms have insisted on the importance of praxis. Truth comes out of the practical involvement in the struggle against injustice and oppression.

Feminist ethics shares much with other forms of liberation theology in that it begins with the experience of oppression. However, Christian feminist ethics differs from South American liberation theology because of its use of Scripture. The feminist experience, unlike the experience of the poor, does not find that much support in the Bible and opposes the patriarchy found in the Scriptures. Since the Catholic tradition was more open to interpreting the Scripture on the basis on reason and experience, Catholic feminists were originally more open to criticize the Scripture than were some Protestant feminist theologians who came out of a *sola Scriptura* background. Feminism, like all liberation theologies, emphasizes the importance of the social location of the person and begins from the concrete experience of oppression. Pre-Vatican II classicism overemphasized universality, underplayed particularity, and often overlooked the oppression of the

poor and minorities. Catholic feminists, in the light
of the catholicity and universality of the Catholic
tradition, still insist on the need for some universal
ethical dimensions despite starting with the experience of the oppression of one group. All people have
to work for the common good. The methodological
and epistemological discussions about universality
and particularity continue.

The new directions in moral theology occasioned
by Vatican II continued to call for further discussion
and elucidation. In addition to the issues already
mentioned, the integration of spirituality and liturgy into moral theology calls for special attention.
Likewise, the role of the human sciences in moral
theology requires more in-depth discussion. Immediately after Vatican II Catholic theology in general
and moral theology in particular were too optimistic
and failed to recognize the continuing reality of
human sinfulness and the fact that the fullness of the
reign of God will only come outside history.
Pre-Vatican II moral theology had overstressed sin
as a particular act but had forgotten about the power
of sin. The experience of the later years since Vatican
II have made theologians more conscious of the
reality of sin both in the world and in the church.

Humanae vitae

Vatican II, as both an event and a symbol, helps to
explain many of the significant changes in Catholic
moral theology in the last forty years of this century.
No other ecclesial event or reality has had a greater

influence on Catholic life and thought. However, *Humanae vitae*, the 1968 encyclical of Pope Paul VI reaffirming the church's condemnation of artificial contraception for spouses, has also greatly affected moral theology.[46]

In the light of Vatican II and the changes associated with it, many Catholics were expecting some change in the papal teaching on artificial contraception. But change did not come. Instead the 1968 encyclical, *Humanae vitae*, set off in the church what its author Paul VI referred to as "a lively discussion."[47] The discussion has centered on two issues— the role of the papal teaching authority and the existence and grounding of moral norms. These two issues have occasioned the most extensive discussion in Catholic moral theology since Vatican II.

The practical aspect of authoritative papal teaching comes to the fore in the question of the legitimacy of dissent by Catholics and by Catholic theologians from the papal teaching on specific moral issues, which the vast majority of Catholic moral theologians claim belong to the category of noninfallible teachings. Some theologians (e.g., Germain Grisez, John Ford) have argued that the teaching on artificial contraception is infallible on the basis of the ordinary infallible teaching of all the bishops together with the pope down through the centuries.[48] The majority deny such infallibility because of the very nature of the object of such teaching (a specific moral norm based on natural law which is not a matter of faith) and the impossibility of proving that the popes and bishops taught this norm as something infallible to be definitively held by all

Catholics. Such teaching could be wrong, and theoretical and practical dissent could be legitimate.[49] Note how this whole issue of authoritative hierarchical teaching in moral matters is primarily an ecclesiological issue, but the moral theologians have had to grapple with it.

At the time of *Humanae vitae*, some significant national conferences of bishops recognized the legitimacy of dissent both by Catholics in general and by theologians although none of the statements from individual bishops' conferences themselves dissented from or disagreed with the papal teaching.[50] Since that time theological and practical dissent has included other papal moral teachings such as sterilization, homosexuality, divorce, the beginning of human life, and the distinction between direct and indirect as found in the manuals.

However, the papal teaching office has continued to insist on all these norms. Pope John Paul II wrote two encyclicals—*Veritatis splendor* (1993) and *Evangelium vitae* (1995)—on these issues showing the importance of intrinsically evil acts based on the object of the act apart from the circumstances and the intention or end of the agent.[51] Since *Humanae vitae* the papal teaching office has never explicitly recognized the possibility of dissent, has taken disciplinary action against many theologians who have dissented from papal teaching especially in the area of sexuality, and has even insinuated that some of these teachings are infallible. In addition, a number of steps have been taken to give the pope and the Roman curia greater control over theologians and their teaching. While some theologians are in agreement with the recent papal declarations and actions, many have disagreed.[52]

Theological disagreement with the way in which papal teaching on morality is exercised has focussed on a number of problems—the lack of broad and deep consultation, the continued reliance on only one theological and philosophical school and methodology, the claim to too great a certitude on specific moral issues, and the unwillingness to admit that some past hierarchical teaching has been erroneous.

The controversy about the moral norm condemning artificial contraception occasioned further discussion about the existence and grounding of moral norms. Revisionist theologians, often called proportionalists, object to describing the object of the moral act in terms of the physical structure of the act and claim that a proportionate reason justifies doing a physical or premoral evil.[53] The school of Germain Grisez and John Finnis has developed their own theory, which differs from the neoscholastic approach, to defend the present moral teaching of the papacy.[54] *Humanae vitae* and its aftermath have thus brought to the fore the two most prominent controversies in Catholic moral theology at the end of the twentieth century.

II. Academic Aspects

Major developments in the academic setting of moral theology occurred as the twentieth century progressed with significant consequences for the discipline. Various factors such as professors and their training, students and the schools in which they are taught, journals, publications, and academic associations contribute to the academic nature of the discipline of moral theology.

Pre-Vatican II

Seminary setting. Until the beginning of Vatican II (1962), the primary home of moral theology was the seminary in which priest professors used the manuals of moral theology to teach future priests how to fulfill their role as judges in the sacrament of penance. At the end of the nineteenth century there was come creativity and critical thinking about moral theology and even about seminary training, but the twentieth century was marked by caution, fear of the new, strong adherence to the manuals, and repetition of what had been accepted in the past.

Rome had begun to take a greater role in the overseeing of seminaries throughout the world in the nineteenth century, but this greatly expanded in the twentieth century. With the condemnation of modernism in the first decade of the twentieth century, all church officials and all seminary personnel had to take the oath against modernism. Neoscholasticism was imposed as the theology and philosophy in seminaries. In this climate the manuals of dogmatic and moral theology continued in existence with little or no dialogue with the modern world. Throughout the twentieth century, Rome, through the curial congregation dealing with seminaries, controlled the spiritual, disciplinary, and intellectual life of the seminary. There was no real intellectual ethos; the primary emphasis was on formation. At best, seminaries were professional schools training people for the ministry. The primary responsibility of the students was to memorize the content of the manuals. A strict lecture system was followed with lectures often being given in Latin at least in the beginning of the century. There was usually no outside reading beyond the textbook for the course, and the students were not required to do research papers. After completing their seminary years, the students usually did not receive any kind of academic or even professional degree.[55] In this context the manuals of moral theology remained firmly entrenched in American Catholic seminaries until Vatican II.

Professors. Some change did take place as the century progressed with regard to the training of professors. Aloysius Sabetti, who wrote the most widely used textbook of American origin in Catholic seminaries, had no special training beyond the regular theology course when he began to teach moral theology at the Woodstock Theologate of the Society of Jesus in Maryland. In fact, Sabetti was at Woodstock learning English in preparation for doing missionary work among the Indians in New Mexico when he was appointed to the faculty of Woodstock as a professor.[56] Only at the end of the nineteenth century did the religious communities of Sulpicians and Vincentians, two groups that were heavily involved in seminary work, send their men for advanced degrees.[57]

In 1929, two American Dominicans, Charles J. Callan and John A. McHugh, published a two-volume moral theology. The two authors, both of whom had advanced degrees from the University of Fribourg in Switzerland, were then teaching at the Maryknoll School of Theology and had collaborated in writing sixteen books on theology, Scripture, and liturgy. They did not pretend to be professionals in any one discipline such as moral theology, but they covered all the areas of theology, philosophy, and Scripture.[58]

One would expect a more scholarly and academic approach to be associated with The Catholic University of America which officially opened in 1889. Thomas Bouquillon (d. 1902), the Belgian-born, first holder of the Chair of Moral Theology at this institution, which was not a seminary but a university dedicated to graduate work, was a true scholar who strongly supported the neoscholasticism of the time.[59] His most famous student at Catholic University was John A. Ryan, a priest of St. Paul, Minnesota, whose influential doctoral dissertation, *A Living Wage*, was published in 1906. Ryan returned to his alma mater to teach moral theology in 1915 and a year later published his *Distributive Justice*. These were Ryan's most scholarly publications. From 1919 until 1944, he served as Director of the Social Action Department of the National Catholic Welfare Conference. He was thus involved in many practical pursuits but continued to give lectures and write essays on many of the problems of the day dealing with social justice which were then often collected into books. Ironically, once Ryan came to Catholic

University to teach, his life and work were less scholarly than before.[60]

Catholic University had many growing pains in the first part of the twentieth century, and Ryan had few graduate students. In fact, in the first fifty years of its existence Catholic University granted just over fifty degrees in all theological disciplines including history of theology, Scripture, dogmatic theology, and moral theology.[61] Those priests who taught in American theologates and seminaries most often went to Europe, but before 1932 Roman doctorates in theology could be obtained in the normal seminary course of four years of theology. There were no requirements for a dissertation involving original research.[62] Thus, many people were teaching moral theology in the United States who had no real graduate work in the discipline.

Publication of scholarly works helps to promote the academic aspects of the discipline. But there were few scholarly publications in moral theology at the time. The immigrant church, concentrating on the professional training of future clerics, with the cloud of the condemnation of modernism hanging over its head, was not really interested in the academic aspects of moral theology. During this fifty year period there were two journals published primarily for priests in this country—*The American Ecclesiastical Review* and the *Homiletic and Pastoral Review*. Both journals frequently published moral cases in which solutions were given to the problems that might come to the priest in confession. Five volumes entitled *The Casuist* brought together many of the cases that were discussed in the *Homiletic and*

Pastoral Review.[63] The Dominican Fathers Callan and McHugh had become joint editors of the *Homiletic and Pastoral Review* in 1916 and continued in that capacity for thirty-four years. At this time there were no truly academic journals of theology in this country.[64]

Beginning about 1940, a move began in the direction of a greater emphasis on the academic aspects of moral theology. Two factors especially occasioned the development—the beginning of more academic associations and scholarly journals and the role of The Catholic University of America. About this time a number of more scholarly journals began. In 1939, the fledgling Catholic Biblical Association began publishing *The Catholic Biblical Quarterly.* The Canon Law Society of America was formed in 1939, and in 1940 the faculty of canon law at The Catholic University of America began publishing *The Jurist.* The Catholic Theological Society of American did not begin until 1946. However, the Dominican Fathers began publishing *The Thomist* in 1939 and the Jesuits started *Theological Studies* in 1940.[65] Thus, the forming of associations and the beginning of more scholarly journals publishing theological articles assisted the move to a more academic approach to theology.

The situation at The Catholic University of America changed perceptibly around 1940. The Second World War made it impossible to send students to Rome to study. Catholic University was now the only available place for future seminary professors to pursue a pontifical or ecclesiastical doctoral degree. (These are degrees accredited by the

Vatican.) This very year coincided with the arrival at Catholic University of the Redemptorist Father Francis J. Connell (1888-1967) to teach moral theology, although he had not previously taught moral theology. Connell wrote a doctoral dissertation for the well-known neoscholastic, Reginald Garrigou-Lagrange, O.P., on the knowledge of Christ; he taught dogmatic theology at the Redemptorist theologate at Esopus, New York, from 1915 to 1940, and contributed many articles and reviews of recent literature on dogmatic theology to the *American Ecclesiastical Review*.[66] From 1941 to 1950, Connell directed about twenty-five dissertations in moral theology at Catholic University.[67] After the war many future seminary professors continued to go to Catholic University to study moral theology under Connell because he had already established a reputation there and built up the tradition of the institution in moral theology. The dissertations he directed dealt with all areas of moral theology but concentrated on particular problems involving sexual and medical ethics. These dissertations were all published and thus gave Catholic University a worldwide reputation in moral theology. Connell also continued the tradition of responding to moral cases in the *American Ecclesiastical Review* from 1944 to 1957 covering 883 questions in that time, in *The Catholic Nurse* from 1953 to 1967, and in *Liguorian* from 1954 until 1967. He published two editions of *Outlines of Moral Theology* (1953 and 1958), left behind an unpublished manuscript "Moral Theology" dated 1962, but never published a real monograph in moral theology.[68]

Connell was clearly a convinced neoscholastic, a theological conservative, a defender of the manuals, and an advocate of a strong papal role in moral theology; but he was a scholar who trained other scholars and provided a more academic environment for moral theology.

At about the same time as Connell, two American Jesuits, Gerald A. Kelly and John C. Ford, also contributed to a more academic approach to moral theology. Both of them did their doctoral dissertations in sexual ethics in Rome in the 1930s, came back to teach in Jesuit theologates in the United States, and developed the discipline of moral theology especially by their articles and overviews of moral theology in *Theological Studies*. From 1941 to 1954 these "Notes on Moral Theology" provided an overview, analysis, and criticism of developments in moral theology throughout the world.[69]

Gerald A. Kelly (1902-1964) wrote primarily in the areas of sexual and especially medical morality. His more scholarly articles appeared in *Theological Studies*, but he also wrote more practical articles for *Health Progress*, the journal of the Catholic Health Association, *The Linacre Quarterly*, the journal of the Catholic Physicians Guild, and *The Review for Religious* to which he also contributed editorial work. He worked closely with the Catholic Health Association in drawing up in 1949 "The Code of Ethical and Religious Directives for Catholic Hospitals" which was expanded in a second edition in 1956. *The Good Confessor* (1951) served as a popular practical pastoral guide for the confessor.[70] Kelly defended the manuals of moral theology, invariably cited the positions taken on issues by older manualists, and staunchly defended the condemnation of artificial contraception.

John C. Ford (1902-1989) was a scholar trained in moral theology at the doctoral level who devoted his life to the teaching and writing of moral theology.[71] Ford recognized and accepted the fact that moral theology was closely associated with canon law. His own preparation in Rome had involved as much canon law as it did moral theology.[72] To deepen his own approach to moral theology he earned a law degree from Boston College in 1941 precisely because morality and law were so closely connected. Ford also developed an interest in psychiatry and psychology—these were areas explored by a number of Catholic scholars at the time—for his work on alcoholism and the psychological evaluation of candidates for religious life.[73] From the time of his doctoral dissertation Ford directed a good part of his time to issues of sexuality. He strongly supported the papal teaching on artificial contraception and, in the last years of his life, insisted that such teaching is infallible by reason of the ordinary magisterium of all the bishops throughout the world together with the pope proposing this teaching as something to be held definitively by Catholics.[74]

Based on their articles in *Theological Studies*, Ford and Kelly planned a series of volumes on contemporary moral theology, two of which were ultimately published on fundamental moral theology and marriage.[75] These works show their knowledge of worldwide developments in moral theology but also their commitment to the manuals of moral theology, and

the decisive importance of the papal teaching office
to determine the morality of particular controversial
issues. Moral theology in pre-Vatican II America
remained primarily a seminary discipline training
future priests, but as the century progressed professors became more academic in their approach to the
discipline, scholarly journals and associations came
into existence, and graduate education at The Catholic University of America prospered.

Post-Vatican II

Dramatic developments in the academic nature of
moral theology occurred beginning about 1960.
Many of these changes came in the wake of Vatican
II, but other influences were also present.

A new setting. The most significant change involved the shift from the professional setting of the
seminary to include and even emphasize the academic setting of colleges and universities. Professors
of moral theology were no longer just clerics or
religious but included the vast majority of lay people,
all of whom were characterized primarily by their
academic interest.

Most people assume that Catholic theology had
been the center of the curriculum in Catholic colleges in the United States in the first half of the
twentieth century, but such was not the case. In the
first half of the century religion or theology was often
not a regular part of the academic curriculum receiv-
ing academic credit. Neoscholastic philosophy was
at the core and center of Catholic colleges, and many

claimed this philosophy constituted the direction and unifying force in the Catholic college curriculum.[76] However, in the 1950s religion courses attracted some attention. Religion teachers at that time were divided between two approaches. The "religion approach" associated with the Dominican Order and others emphasized the speculative nature of the discipline and generally followed the different tracts or subject matters of the neoscholastic manuals of theology. The "theology approach" stressed theology's relationship primarily to the student and saw the discipline as motivating the student to live the Christian life and to become a lay apostle. Such an approach stressed the difference between theology for priests and theology for the Catholic laity who would be taught in Catholic colleges.[77]

Despite these debates among the elite, on a practical level religion courses in Catholic colleges were often little more than catechism classes taught by priests or religious who had no real academic training. Discussions among those teaching religion or theology in Catholic colleges resulted in the formation of The Society of Catholic College Teachers of Sacred Doctrine which held its first meeting at Trinity College in Washington, D.C., in 1955. One of the primary concerns was the quality of undergraduate courses in religion on Catholic campuses. Even the secular accrediting agencies—Catholic colleges in general had become more academic and entered into the mainstream of American colleges by participating in the work of the different regional accrediting agencies—had pointed out that religion courses in Catholic colleges were frequently inad-

equate and superficial in content and failed to meet
the norms demanded for the academic recognition
of other college disciplines. The society was formed
to try to make theology in Catholic colleges a truly
academic discipline on a par with other subjects
taught there.[78]

The academic nature of Catholic theology gradually took on greater importance. One significant
factor was the need to train teachers with the appro-
priate doctorate for their work in teaching theology
on college campuses. For all practical purposes theology had been the province of male clerics and The
Catholic University of American was the only place
in the country conferring doctoral degrees. In 1943
St. Mary's College in South Bend began a program
in theology and twenty-five women, mostly sisters,
received a doctorate.[79] By the 1960s other institutions began to offer doctoral degrees in theology.
Gerard Sloyan, chair of the Department of Religious
Education at Catholic University, and Bernard Cooke
of Marquette were leaders in preparing new Ph.Ds
and working with the Society of Catholic College
Teachers of Sacred Doctrine. Many other institutions now grant Ph.D. degrees in theology—Boston
College, Duquesne University, Fordham University, Loyola University of Chicago, Notre Dame
University, St. Louis University, and the University
of Dayton. At its beginning the Society of Catholic
College Teachers of Sacred Doctrine was primarily
run by clerics and religious, but as time went on
more lay people became involved in the organization. Today the vast majority of professors in Catholic departments of theology are lay.[80]

The emphasis on the academic nature of theology developed together with the changed understanding of Catholic higher education itself. Until the 1960s Catholic higher education saw itself as part of the pastoral arm of the church. However, Catholic higher education was gradually forming closer ties with American higher education in general. By the late 1960s many Catholic leaders in higher education were calling for the autonomy of the Catholic college with regard to any authority, lay or clerical, outside the college and the need for academic freedom. In the 1970s the mainstream of Catholic higher education moved in this direction and restructured their institutions accordingly.[81]

In this context Catholic theology became a truly academic discipline and not just catechetics or the inculcation of Catholic doctrine. The academic freedom of Catholic theology in the academy also meant that church authorities could no longer directly interfere with who was teaching theology in Catholic higher education. Many struggles over academic freedom have taken place in Catholic higher education, but the mainstream of Catholic colleges and universities have strongly supported the academic freedom of Catholic theologians.[82] However, the Vatican has lately insisted on a greater control over theologians in Catholic colleges and universities and no one knows what the future holds in store.[83] Thus today doctorate degrees in theology are granted by many Catholic institutions and qualified professors in undergraduate programs teach theology and/or religious studies as a truly academic discipline on a

par with other curricular offerings. Since many
Catholic colleges require a certain number of hours
in theology, the number of trained theologians has
greatly increased.

Other developments. As theology has become more
academic, significant changes have also occurred on
other levels which support the academic nature of
theology. The Catholic Theological Society of
America (CTSA) has changed dramatically from its
beginning as a group of priest professors of theology
teaching in seminaries. Until 1960 the published
Proceedings began with a photograph of the bishop
of the city in which the convention was held. In
1966 the first woman attended a meeting.[84] Due to
the fact that some well-known theologians associated with more liberal positions played leadership
roles, the CTSA became the dominant academic
theological society. The College Theology Society
(The name changed from the Catholic College
Teachers of Sacred Doctrine in 1967.) has continued to work for a more academic approach to
theology on the college level, and since 1974 has
published a respected scholarly journal, *Horizons.*[85]
In 1977 in reaction to the perceived liberalism of the
other Catholic societies, a number of Catholic scholars in different disciplines formed the Fellowship of
Catholic Scholars with a commitment to uphold the
teaching of the hierarchical magisterium.[86]

The ecumenical aspects of contemporary Catholic
moral theology are very evident. The Society of
Christian Ethics began in 1959 as an association
primarily of professors of social ethics in Protestant
divinity schools. A few Catholics joined in 1963, the

first Catholic president served in 1971, and today a large percentage of the membership is Catholic. Like the CTSA the society has moved from a preponderance of seminary professors to the vast majority now teaching in colleges and universities. This society has also become more academically oriented over the years. The independent *Journal of Religious Ethics* encouraged by the Society of Christian Ethics is a significant scholarly journal begun in 1973.[87] Even more significant from an ecumenical perspective are the number of Catholic scholars who have received their degrees from Protestant and secular universities. James M. Gustafson, both at Yale and at Chicago, directed the dissertations of over twenty well-known Catholic moral theologians.[88] Today Catholic moral theology must be done in the context of ecumenical dialogue.

Both the quantity and quality of professors of moral theology has increased dramatically over the past thirty years of this century. The moral theologians of 1950 would be amazed at the multitude, gender, and academic backgrounds of Catholic moral theologians today. Because of the large number of Catholic colleges and universities in the United States, there are more moral theologians in this country than in any other country in the world. Moral theology in other countries has also become more academic, but the number of professional moral theologians is much less.[89] It is probably safe to say that there are more moral theologians existing today then have existed in the whole history of the discipline before this time. The quality is shown in the many articles and books that have been pub-

lished. Academic scholars are evaluated and promoted on the basis of their publishing, and the
literature in moral theology has dramatically increased. The academic development with its emphasis on depth and research has multiplied the different
number of subspecialties in moral theology. No
longer can one scholar be an expert on all of moral
theology.[90] Professors now have to specialize in one
or other specific area (e.g. fundamental, social, political, economic, sexual, biomedical) or aspect (different periods of history, relationship with a particular
science, philosophical).

Before Vatican II moral theology in the United
States was a Roman-centered and controlled discipline. The most significant moral theologians in the
world in the post-Vatican II period, Bernard Häring
and Joseph Fuchs taught in Rome and had a great
influence precisely because of their base in Rome.
Many of the first generation of post-Vatican II moral
theologians in the United States who are now approaching retirement did their doctoral work in
Rome. But now all that has changed. The Wojtyla
papacy has insisted on a centralized church with
Rome directing all the local churches and has seen
theology functioning in the same way. But the
existential reality is quite different and has contributed to some of the tensions between United States
theologians and the Vatican.

In general the consequences for moral theology
coming from a greater emphasis on the academic
aspects of the discipline have been positive and
productive for moral theology. However, four possible dangers should be recognized now and in the

future. First, moral theology exists in the service of the church and this aspect can never be forgotten.[91] The ecclesial and academic aspects of the discipline must always be in some tension, but the ecclesial aspect cannot be forgotten. Second, the preferential option for the poor and marginalized which should characterize Catholic moral theology today does not always find a hospitable environment in the academy. Third, the existence of a large, vibrant, and academically respectable discipline of moral theology in the United States has resulted in much less dialogue and familiarity with Catholic moral theology in other countries. The Catholic approach must always strive to be universal and should never be limited to the boundaries of any one country, despite the fact that inculturation means moral theology will have significant differences in different countries. Fourth, academically acceptable publication can also be limited to the narrow world of the professoriate and downplay the role of the public intellectual both in society at large and in the church. The role of moral theology contributing intellectually to the life of the church and of the broader society cannot be forsaken.

Radical is the proper adjective to describe the changes in the academic aspects of moral theology since 1960. The quantity, quality, gender, and professional preparation of moral theologians are dramatically changed since 1960. However, further changes are needed especially with regard to bringing Hispanic and minority people into the professoriate.

III. Societal Aspects

Since moral theology deals with issues facing society, social developments will definitely influence the discipline. In the first part of the twentieth century the Catholic Church was an immigrant church, often accused of living in its own ghetto, and not all that concerned about the broader society and its issues. Nevertheless, John A. Ryan not only addressed the social problems facing American society in the first half of the century but also worked with other Americans in trying to bring about social change. Ryan employed a Catholic anthropology emphasizing the social nature of human beings, the common good, a positive role for the state, and distributive justice with its insistence on the importance of human need as a basic criterion of distributing material goods. He frequently worked with the progressive forces for change in society. Many of the causes he championed were later accepted by the New Deal.[92]

John Ford not only discussed the pastoral problem of alcoholism, but he also condemned the saturation bombing of Germany in a very renowned and prophetic article in *Theological Studies* in 1944. Ford argued that such bombing violated the just war criterion of noncombatant immunity.[93]

John Courtney Murray dealt successfully with the most divisive issue facing the Catholic Church in its relationship to the United States—the separation of church and state. In a series of scholarly articles appearing in *Theological Studies,* Murray showed that the American understanding of the separation of church and state was totally compatible with Catholic principles. Murray's original interest was in Catholic action and how Catholic laity can and should cooperate in working with all others for peace and justice. Although Murray was silenced in the mid 1950s, he exerted a strong influence on the Vatican II Declaration on Religious Liberty. Murray argued primarily from the role and function of a limited constitutional government.[94]

Without doubt Murray proposed a lesser role for the state than had John Ryan who wanted a greater role for the state in economic matters but who also accepted the older Catholic approach to religious freedom with its emphasis on a religious role for the state. Ryan's writings on the Catholic teaching on church and state played a significant role in the 1928 presidential campaign of Alfred E. Smith when others pointed out that even a liberal like Ryan could not accept the separation of church and state.[95] In more recent times the cognate issues of law and morality and of religion and politics have come to the fore.[96]

The Second Vatican Council in its Pastoral Constitution on the Church in the Modern World tried to overcome the split between faith and daily life and to see working and living in the world as carrying on the redemptive mission of Jesus.[97] Papal documents and encyclicals have dealt with the social problems of the world, and the United States Catholic bishops have taken a leadership role with their two pastoral letters on peace and the economy with its emphasis on a preferential option for the poor.[98] Many Catholic theologians have supported the general position taken by the United States bishops in calling for some state intervention to make the market economy serve the needs of all, especially the poor, but a school, often called Catholic neoconservatives (e.g. Michael Novak, Richard John Neuhaus, and George Weigel), have proposed a less critical approach to the American scene and American capitalism. Both sides in this debate claim the mantle of John Courtney Murray.[99]

A strong school of Catholic feminist ethicists has come to the fore in the United States. Feminism takes its origin from the reality of patriarchy and the oppression of women, but it is more than just part of the object of ethics. Feminism proposes a new and different methodology for moral theology beginning with the experience of the oppression of women.[100]

Catholic moral theology traditionally has been interested in medical ethics, but since 1970 bioethics has become an important and distinct discipline in philosophy, law, and in religious ethics. In addition to all the new problems raised by newer technologies, the questions of the social distribution of healthcare and its provision have come to the fore. Environmental ethics has also arisen in philosophical and religious ethics including Catholic moral theology in the light of the degradation of the environment. Environmental ethics argues against the one-sided anthropological priority that has often been associated with twentieth century Christian theology in general.

Thus, developments in our society have raised many new issues for moral theology but at the same time also occasioned the rise of newer approaches and methodologies within Catholic moral theology. Catholic moral theology has not always responded well to these societal issues (e.g. race), but societal issues have often set the agenda for moral theology.

IV. CONTINUITIES

Despite the very deep and significant changes that have occurred in this century of moral theology in the United States, important basic continuities have also been present. The Catholic tradition with its emphasis on universality and inclusiveness has been characterized methodologically by its "and"—Scripture and tradition, faith and reason, grace and works, Jesus and the church and Mary and the saints. Closely connected with this emphasis on the "and" has been the acceptance of mediation—the fact that the divine is mediated in and through the human. Mediation supports the Catholic insistence on a fundamental goodness of the human and of human reason.

Even before Vatican II when the Catholic Church saw itself in great opposition with the modern world, moral theology still insisted on the goodness of human reason and its ability to arrive at moral wisdom and truth. The shift at Vatican II from condemnation to dialogue with others and with the world gave new impetus to the traditional role of reason in Catholic moral theology. Above all, this development unlocked Catholic reason from the neoscholastic box in which it had been kept. Moral theology thus is open to dialogue with various philosophical partners. Witness the dialogue between Catholicism and its old enemy liberalism.[101] Catholic moral theology as exemplified by John A. Ryan has traditionally been open to working with other sciences such as economics in dealing with the human issues facing us. Yes, reason can easily be abused especially by power and sin, but the Catholic approach recognizes the role of human reason and with historical consciousness now accepts human experience together with Scripture and tradition. Of course, the critical questions always remain—whose reason and experience and how are they to be tested?

The Catholic concern for all that God has made grounds the traditional Catholic interest in the world and what happens in the broader society. In the light of the traditional distinction between sect (the group that withdraws from the world) and church (the group that stays and works in the world), the Catholic Church remains the best example of a church concerned with the world in which it lives.[102] Individuals and groups within the church can and should be called at times to witness to particular virtues or aspects of the Christian life, but the whole Catholic Church will always have a concern for and an interest in working with all others for a more free, peaceful, just, and sustainable society.

The Catholic moral tradition has been concerned about the morality of particular acts and has appealed to both principles and casuistry in trying to determine the morality of particular acts. The orientation of Catholic moral theology to the work of the confessor as judge accentuated this concern with particular actions, but even without the confessional aspect, the tradition has always given importance to discerning the rightness or wrongness of particular acts. Since the renewal of Vatican II, Catholic moral theology has again recognized the importance of the virtues in moral life. Some have attempted to see virtues, principles, and casuistry as three exclusive methods in ethics, but the Catholic moral tradition has tended to see them as complementary and not exclusive—another example of the Catholic "and."

There is also some continuity in what I consider a negative factor in the Catholic moral tradition—its failure to give enough recognition to the power of sin. An older Catholic moral theology stressed sin as an act, but it forgot about sin as a power affecting both the person and the structures of society. Without doubt, Catholic theology immediately following Vatican II tended to be too optimistic precisely because it failed to give enough importance to the reality of sin. While making sure that Catholic moral theology recognizes the reality of sin, I never want to so emphasize sin that it destroys the human.

Catholic anthropology in this century has definitely shifted toward the subject and the person, but the Catholic tradition continues to insist that the person lives in social relationships with others and is not an isolated individual. Perhaps the greatest difference between the Catholic approach and the approach often found in contemporary American life centers on this question of individualism. The Catholic tradition sees the individual as intimately related to particular human beings (e.g. family) and ultimately related to all in the human community.

By recognizing the social nature of the individual, the Catholic tradition is not opposed to human happiness or fulfillment but claims that this happiness or fulfillment comes to the person not as an isolated individual, but as one living in these multiple relationships and communities, including the state. The principle of subsidiarity and the recognition of a positive but limited role for the state continue to characterize Catholic social ethics. Today the relational understanding of the person must also include the relationship to the environment.

Since Vatican II and the rise of liberation theology, Catholic theology has recognized a preferential option for the poor. However, the concern for the poor and the needy has been a perennial Christian concern. Such a concern provided the impetus for much of John A. Ryan's approach. Today, as we are more conscious of the inequalities of wealth and power in our country and in our world, this concern for the poor and the marginalized has become more central.

There can be no doubt that the Catholic tradition has generally not given enough importance to diversity in all its forms. Beginning with a move to historical consciousness at Vatican II and continuing in liberation and feminist ethics, social location and diverse starting places for ethics have become much more common. Such starting places at times are absolutely necessary in order to give due importance to the marginalized and their experience. However, the Roman Catholic tradition, as well illustrated in contemporary Catholic feminist thought, still recognizes the need for a morality that has some universal aspects and recognizes the social and global aspects of all we do today.[103] In the past the Catholic tradition overstressed universality and what was held in common, but the need for some universality and communality will always be a part of the Catholic moral tradition.

This section has briefly indicated some of the significant continuities in the Catholic ethical tradition even amid the dramatic changes of the twentieth century. In general I believe there will always be a distinctive Catholic tradition in moral theology, but that tradition itself will also be open to change and development over time. The danger in the future might be that Catholic moral theologians will not be as familiar with the Catholic moral tradition and its historical development.

Conclusion. This lecture has tried to analyze the deep changes in Catholic moral theology in the United States in the twentieth century in the light of the three publics served by moral theology—the church, the academy, and the broader society. However, despite all these changes, some continuities continue to exist precisely because there is a distinctive Catholic way of doing ethics which itself is also open to development.

At the end of the century people are inclined to look both backward and forward. This essay has looked backward, but the curious will ask: What will happen in the next century or even in the next millennium?

In the light of the changes that occurred in twentieth century Catholic moral theology, no one writing in 1899 could have ever predicted what would occur in the twentieth century precisely because of the unforeseen historical developments that influenced so many of the changes. For this same reason, I do not think that anyone today can accurately predict or forecast what will happen to moral theology in the next century. What will happen will be deeply imbedded in the historical and cultural changes affecting the church, the academy, and the broader human society.

NOTES

1. Thomas Bouquillon, "Moral Theology at the End of the Nineteenth Century," *Catholic University Bulletin* 5 (1899): 244-68.
2. James M. Gustafson, review of *The Origins of Moral Theology in the United States: Three Different Approaches* and *Feminist Ethics and the Catholic Moral Tradition: Readings in Moral Theology No. 9, America,* 117 n.11 (October 18, 1997): 26.
3. For the most widely used manual of moral theology written in the United States, see Aloysius Sabetti, *Compendium theologiae moralis*, 34th ed., ed. Daniel F. Creeden (New York: Pustet, 1939).
4. Bouquillon, *Catholic University Bulletin* 5 (1899): 244-68.
5. John B. Hogan, *Clerical Studies* (Boston: Marlier, Callanan, 1898), pp. 197-262.
6. John Talbot Smith, *An Essay on Clerical Training* (New York: William H. Young, 1896), pp. 266-71.
7. Joseph M. White, *The Diocesan Seminary in the United States: A History from the 1780s to the Present* (Notre Dame, Ind.: University of Notre Dame Press, 1989), pp. 367-68; 380-81. See also John C. Boere, "A Survey of the Content and Organization of the Curriculum of the Theological Department of Major Seminaries in the United States of America" (M.A. diss., The Catholic University of America, 1963).

8 James W. O'Brien, "The Scientific Teaching of Moral Theology," *Proceedings of the Catholic Theological Society of America* 4 (1949): 193-95.

9. R. Scott Appleby, *Church and Age Unite: The Modernist Impulse in American Catholicism* (Notre Dame, Ind.: University of Notre Dame Press, 1992), pp. 196-206; Michael V. Gannon, "Before and After Modernism: The Intellectual Isolation of the American Priest," in *The Catholic Priest in the United States: Historical Investigations*, ed. John Tracy Ellis (Collegeville, Minn.: St. John's University Press, 1971), pp. 293-383. Appleby unlike Gannon sees a definite connection between Americanism and Modernism.

10. J.A. Weisheipl, "Scholasticism," *New Catholic Encyclopedia* 12, pp. 1167-168.

11. Bouquillon, *Catholic University Bulletin* 5 (1899): 244-68.

12. Marciano Vidal, *La morale di Sant' Alfonso: Dal rigorismo alla benignità* (Rome: Editiones Academiae Alphonsianae, 1992), p. 201. For the best and latest English language biography of Alphonsus, see Frederick M. Jones, *Alphonsus de Liguori: The Saint of Bourbon Naples 1696-1787* (Westminster, Md.: Christian Classics, 1992).

13. Ph. Lecrivain, "St. Alphonse aux risques du rigorisme et du liguorisme," *Studia Moralia* 25 (1987): 386-94; Vidal, *La morale di Sant' Alfonso*, pp.201-16.

14. John A. Ryan, "The Immorality of Contraception," *American Ecclesiastical Review* 75 (1928): 408-11; "Comment by Dr. Ryan," *American Ecclesiastical Review* 81 (1929): 70-72.

15. John A. Ryan, *Seven Troubled Years 1930-36: A Collection of Papers on the Depression and on the Problems of Recovery and Reform* (Ann Arbor, Mich.: Edwards Brothers, 1937), p. 59. For my analysis of Ryan's principle of expediency, see my *American Catholic Social Ethics: Twentieth Century Approaches* (Notre Dame, Ind.: University of Notre Dame Press, 1982), pp. 38-41, 87-88.

16. Ryan, *American Ecclesiastical Review* 81 (1929): 71-72.

17. William B. Smith, "Selected Methodological Questions in the Fundamental Moral Theology of Francis J. Connell, C.SS.R.," (S.T.D. diss., The Catholic University of American, 1971), pp. 249-56.

18. Gerald A. Kelly, "The Morality of Artificial Insemination," *American Ecclesiastical Review* 101 (1939): 101-19. For a helpful discussion of Kelly's life and work, see Edwin L. Lisson, "The Historical Context and Sources of Moral Theology in the Writings of Gerald A. Kelly, S.J.," (S.T.D. diss., Pontifical Gregorian University, 1975).

19. Gerald A. Kelly, "Notes on Moral Theology," *Theological Studies* 11 (1950): 68. See also Kelly, *Medico-Moral Problems* (St. Louis, Mo.: Catholic Hospital Association, 1958), pp. 242-43.

20. John R. Connery, *Abortion: The Development of the Roman Catholic Perspective* (Chicago, Ill.: Loyola University Press, 1977), pp. 225-303.

21. *Curriculum of the Major Seminary in Relation to Contemporary Conditions* (Washington, D.C.: National Catholic Welfare Conference, 1935), pp. 46-47.

22. Aloysius Sabetti, *Compendium Theologiae Moralis*, 7th ed. (New York: Pustet, 1892).

23. Kelly, *Medico-Moral Problems*, p. 363.

24. John C. Ford and Gerald Kelly, *Contemporary Moral Theology*, vol. 1, *Questions in Fundamental Moral Theology* (Westminster, Md.: Newman, 1958); *Contemporary Moral Theology*, vol. 2, *Marriage Questions* (Westminster, Md.: Newman, 1963). The original title proposed for this work was "Moral Theology under Pius XII." See Lisson, "Historical Context," p. 188.

25. Lisson, "Historical Context," pp. 216-99.

26. Henricus Denzinger, et. al., eds., *Enchiridion symbolorum definitionum et declarationum de rebus fidei et morum*, 32nd ed., (Barcelona: Herder, 1963), nn. 3384-385.

27. Ford and Kelly, *Contemporary Moral Theology*, vol. 1, pp. 19-41.

28. Ford and Kelly, *Contemporary Moral Theology*, vol. 2, pp. 235-459; see also Kelly, "Contraception and Natural Law," *Proceedings of the Catholic Theological Society of America* 18 (1963): 27-28.

29. John C. Ford and Germain Grisez, "Contraception and the Infallibility of the Ordinary Magisterium," *Theological Studies* 39 (1978): 258-312; for Ford's growing emphasis on the

authoritative teaching against contraception, see Margaret Kelly Menius, "John Cuthbert Ford, S.J.: His Contribution to Twentieth Century Catholic Moral Theology on the Issue of Contraception," (Ph.D. diss., St. Louis University, 1998).

30. Francis L. Broderick, "The Encyclicals and Social Action: Is John A. Ryan Typical?" *Catholic Historical Review* 55 (1969): 1-6.

31. Francis L. Broderick, *Right Reverend New Dealer: John A. Ryan* (New York: Macmillan, 1963).

32. John A. Ryan, *A Living Wage: Its Ethical and Economical Aspects* (New York: Macmillan, 1906); Ryan, *Distributive Justice: The Right and Wrong of our Present Distribution of Wealth* (New York: Macmillan, 1916). This 431 page book cites Leo XIII on only six pages—64-66, 306, 309, 377.

33. For my analysis of Ryan, see Curran, *American Catholic Social Ethics*, pp. 28-91.

34. John F. Cronin, *Social Principles and Economic Life* (Milwaukee, Wis.: Bruce, 1959) p. vii.

35. John F. Cronin, "Forty Years Later: Reflections and Reminiscences," *American Ecclesiastical Review* 164 (1971): 314-15.

36. Bernhard Häring, *Das Gesetz Christi: Moral theologie dargestellt für Priester und Laien* (Freiburg, i.Br: Erich Wewel, 1954).

37. Ford and Kelly, *Contemporary Moral Theology*, vol. 1, pp. 80-103.

38. Examples of the second school include Patristic scholars such as Jean Daniélou, Henri de Lubac, Hans Urs von Balthazar, Louis Bouyer, and Joseph Ratzinger.

39. Bernard Lonergan, "The Transition from a Classicist Worldview to Historical Mindedness," in *Law for Liberty: The Role of Law in the Church Today*, ed. James E. Biechler (Baltimore, Md.: Helicon, 1967), pp. 126-33.

40. Pastoral Constitution on the Church in the Modern World, n. 12, in *Vatican Council II: The Conciliar and Post-Conciliar Documents*, ed. Austin Flannery (Collegeville, Minn.: Liturgical, 1992), p. 913.

41. Declaration on Religious Liberty, n. 2, in *Vatican Council II*, ed. Flannery, p. 800.

42. E.g., Albert C. Outler, *Methodist Observer at Vatican II* (Westminster, Md.: Newman, 1967).

43. Decree on the Training of Priests, n. 16, in *Vatican Council II*, ed. Flannery, p. 720.

44. Pastoral Constitution on the Church in the Modern World, n.43, in *Vatican Council II*, ed. Flannery, p. 943.

45. Most of the observations and controversies mentioned in the subsequent paragraphs are discussed in detail in the eleven volume series, *Readings in Moral Theology*, ed. Charles E. Curran and Richard A. McCormick (New York: Paulist, 1979-1999). No specific references will be given in the following paragraphs.

46. Pope Paul VI, *The Regulation of Birth: Humanae vitae* (Washington, D.C.: U.S. Catholic Conference, 1968).

47. Paul VI used the expression, "la vívida discussión" in a speech delivered to the Second General Conference of Latin American Bishops (CELAM) held at Medellín, Colombia, on August 24, 1968. *Acta Apostolicae Sedis* 60 (1968): 649.

48. Ford and Grisez, *Theological Studies* 39 (1978): 258-312.

49. For the different positions in this debate, see *Readings in Moral Theology No.6: Dissent in the Church*, ed. Charles E. Curran and Richard A. McCormick (New York: Paulist, 1988). For a defense of the majority position, see Francis A. Sullivan, *Magisterium: Teaching Authority in the Catholic Church* (New York: Paulist, 1983); Sullivan, *Creative Fidelity: Weighing and Interpreting Documents of the Magisterium* (New York: Paulist, 1996). For the differences between Grisez and Sullivan, see Francis A. Sullivan, "'The Secondary Object' of Infallibility," *Theological Studies* 54 (1993): 536-50; Grisez and Sullivan, "The Ordinary Magisterium's Infallibility," *Theological Studies* 55 (1994): 720-38.

50. William H. Shannon, *The Lively Debate* pp. 117-146; Joseph A. Selling, "The Reaction to *Humanae vitae*," pp. 1-139.

51. Pope John Paul II, *Veritatis splendor*, *Origins* 23 (1993): 297-334; John Paul II, *Evangelium vitae*, *Origins* 24 (1995): 689-727.

52. For my discussion of these issues, see Charles E. Curran, *The Catholic Moral Tradition Today: A Synthesis* (Washington, D.C.: Georgetown University Press, 1999), Chapter 8.

53. Bernard Hoose, *Proportionalism: The American Debate and Its European Roots* (Washington, D.C.: Georgetown University Press, 1987). For an overview of the approach of Richard A. McCormick, the most prominent American proponent of proportionalism, see Paulinus Ikechukwu Odozor, *Richard A. McCormick and The Renewal of Moral Theology* (Notre Dame, Ind.: University of Notre Dame Press, 1995).

54. Germain Grisez is a prolific scholar who is now writing a multi-volume textbook of moral theology. See especially Germain Grisez, *The Way of the Lord Jesus*, vol. 1, *Christian Moral Principles* (Chicago, Ill.: Franciscan Herald, 1983); for a succinct and accurate summary of his basic thesis see Germain Grisez and Russell Shaw, *Fulfillment in Christ: A Summary of Christian Moral Principles* (Notre Dame, Ind.: University of Notre Dame Press, 1991); John Finnis, *Fundamentals of Ethics* (Washington, D.C.: Georgetown University Press, 1983).

55. White, *The Diocesan Seminary*, pp. 265-92. Gannon, in *The Catholic Priest in the United States*, ed. Ellis, pp. 293-383. For the story of the seminary of the archdiocese of New York that had been in the forefront of academic work in the early twentieth century, see Thomas J. Shelly, *Dunwoodie: The History of St. Joseph's Seminary Yonkers NY* (Westminster, Md.: Christian Classics, 1993), pp. 172ff.

56. Patrick J. Dooley, *Woodstock and Its Makers* (Woodstock, Md.: College Press, 1927), pp. 86-89; "Father Aloisius Sabetti," *Woodstock Letters* 29 (1900): 208-13. This autobiographical article was written by Sabetti at the request of the editor of *Woodstock Letters* and published after his death. All the professors were asked to write such autobiographies.

57. White, *Diocesan Seminary*, p. 257.

58. J. Coffey, "Callan, Charles Jerome," in *New Catholic Encyclopedia*, 15 vols. (New York: McGraw Hill, 1967), 2, pp. 1077-78; "J. Coffey, "McHugh, John Ambrose," *New*

Catholic Encyclopedia, 9, p. 34; John Langlois "Callan, Charles Jerome (1877-1962)," in *The Encyclopedia of American Catholic History*, ed. Michael Glazier and Thomas J. Shelley (Collegeville, Minn.: Liturgical, 1997) p. 194; Langlois, "McHugh, John Ambrose (1880-1950)," in *The Encyclopedia of American Catholic History*, p. 887.

59. Charles E. Curran, *Origins of Moral Theology in the United States: Three Different Approaches* (Washington, D.C.: Georgetown University Press, 1997), pp. 171-254.

60. Broderick, *Right Reverend New Dealer*: Curran, *American Catholic Social Ethics*, pp. 26-91.

61. School of Religious Studies, The Catholic University of America, *A Century of Religious Studies: Faculty and Dissertations* (Washington, D.C.: Catholic University of America Press, 1989), pp. 23-25; for the history, see C. Joseph Nuesse, *The Catholic University of America: A Centennial History* (Washington, D.C.: Catholic University of America Press, 1990); White, *Diocesan Seminary*, pp. 318-335.

62. White, *Diocesan Seminary*, pp. 277-78.

63. *The Casuist: A Collection of Cases in Moral and Pastoral Theology*, 5 vols. (New York: Joseph F. Wagner, 1906-1917).

64. R. Scott Appleby, "American Ecclesiastical Review," in *Religious Periodicals of the United States*, ed. Charles H. Lippy (Westport, Conn.: Greenwood, 1986), pp. 21-25; Bernard Noone, "Homiletic and Pastoral Review," in *Religious Periodicals*, ed. Lippy, pp. 245-49.

65. Robert J. Wister, "Theology in America" in *Encyclopedia of American Catholic History*, p. 1382.

66. William B. Smith, "Selected Methodological Questions," pp. 1-31.

67. The Catholic University of America, *A Century of Religious Studies*, pp. 26-33.

68. Smith, "Selected Methodological Questions," pp. 32-54. For Connell's position on the immorality of professional prize fighting, see Francis J. Connell, "Prize Fighting and Boxing," *American Ecclesiastical Review* 122 (1950): 58-59. Connell also directed a dissertation on this subject: George C. Bernard, *The Morality of Prize Fighting* (Washington, D.C.: Catholic University of America Press, 1952).

69. For studies of Kelly and Ford, see Lisson, "Historical Context" and Margaret Kelly Menius, "John Cuthbert Ford."

70. Lisson, "Historical Context," pp. 154-209. Kelly also wrote a well used book on medical ethics commenting on the directives—Gerald Kelly, *Medico-Moral Problems* (St. Louis, Mo.: Catholic Health Association, 1958). American Catholic authors at this time were writing a number of works in medical ethics often as textbooks for students. Gerald Kelly, *The Good Confessor* (New York: Sentinel, 1951).

71. For an overview of Ford's life and work, see Menius, "John Cuthbert Ford," pp. 94-140.

72. Lisson, "Historical Context," pp. 145-46. One of Ford's books was a canonical commentary, John C. Ford, *The New Eucharistic Legislation: A Commentary on the Apostolic Constitution Christus Dominus and on the Instruction of the Holy Office on the Discipline to be Observed Concerning the Eucharistic Fast* (New York: P.J. Kennedy, 1953).

73. John C. Ford, *Man Takes a Drink: Facts and Principles about Alcohol* (New York: P.J. Kennedy, 1965); Ford, *Religious Superiors, Subjects, and Psychiatrists* (Westminster, Md.: Newman, 1963).

74. Menius, "John Cuthbert Ford," pp. 143-291.

75. John C. Ford and Gerald Kelly, *Contemporary Moral Theology,* vol. 1, *Questions in Moral Theology* and vol. 2, *Marriage Questions.*

76. Philip Gleason, *Contending with Modernity: Catholic Higher Education in the Twentieth Century* (New York: Oxford University Press, 1995), pp. 163-66. Very little has been written on the historical development of Catholic college theology. For a helpful overview of the aims of college theology, see Patrick W. Carey, "College Theology in Historical Perspective," in *American Catholic Traditions: Resources for Renewal,* ed. Sandra Yocum Mize and William L. Portier, Annual Publication of the College Theology Society 1996, vol. 42 (Maryknoll, N.Y.: Orbis, 1997) pp. 242-71.

77. Charles E. Sheedy, "The Problem of Theology for the Laity," *Proceedings of the Catholic Theological Society of*

America 7 (1952): 111-24; Gleason, *Contending with Modernity*, pp. 256-60.

78. Rosemary Rodgers, *A History of the College Theology Society* (Villanova, Penn.: College Theology Society c/o Horizons, 1983), pp. 11-12.

79. Gleason, *Contending with Modernity*, pp. 258-59. Since the 1930s the Department of Religious Education at Catholic University could grant Ph.D.s to nonclerics and women, but as a matter of fact very few such degrees were earned before the late 1950s.

80. Carey, in *American Catholic Traditions*, ed. Mize and Portier, pp. 259-61; Rodgers, *History of the College Theology Society*.

81. Alice Gallin, *Independence and a New Partnership in Catholic Higher Education* (Notre Dame, Ind.: University of Notre Dame Press, 1996).

82. For my discussion of these issues, see Charles E. Curran, *Catholic Higher Education, Theology, and Academic Freedom* (Notre Dame, Ind.: University of Notre Dame Press, 1990).

83. Pope John Paul II, *Ex corde Ecclesiae, Origins* 20 (1990): 265-76; Ex corde Ecclesiae Implementation Committee, "Ex corde Ecclesiae: An Application to the United States," a sub-committee report submitted for discussion at the November 1998 meeting of the National Conference of Catholic Bishops.

84. "CTSA Firsts," *Proceedings of the Catholic Theological Society of America* 50 (1995): 293-98.

85. Rodgers, *History of the College Theology Society*.

86. James Hitchcock, "The Fellowship of Catholic Scholars," in *Being Right: Conservative Catholics in America*, ed. Mary Jo Weaver and R. Scott Appleby (Bloomington, Ind.: University of Indiana Press, 1995), pp. 186-210.

87. Edward Le Roy Long, *Academic Bonding and Social Concern: The Society of Christian Ethics, 1959-1983* (Notre Dame, Ind.: Religious Ethics, 1984).

88. Personal Communication from James M. Gustafson, November 9, 1998.

89. In France, for example, the journal published by the Dominican Order in France now called *Revue d' éthique et*

de théologie morale: Le Supplément is associated with ATEM—the French Speaking Ecumenical Association of Moral Theologians: See "Dossier: Un demi-siècle avec La Revue," *Revue d'éthique et de théologie morale: Le Supplément* n.203 (Décembre 1997): 5-187. In Italy *Rivista di teologia morale* began publishing four times a year in 1969 in association with ATISM, the Italian Theological Association for the Study of Moral Theology.

90. Richard A. McCormick wrote the "Notes on Moral Theology" for *Theological Studies* from 1965 to 1984 in which he reviewed, analyzed, and criticized the periodical literature in all of moral theology and in many different languages. Since that time different moral theologians have treated different aspects of moral theology in the "Notes on Moral Theology." No longer can any one person be in dialogue with all the literature (even limited to the periodical literature) in all languages on all aspects of moral theology.

91. No one in the United States today writes extensively on moral theology from a more pastoral and ecclesial perspective. For an example of this type of writing in England, see Kevin T. Kelly, *New Directions in Moral Theology: The Challenge of Being Human* (London: G. Chapman, 1992); Kelly, *New Directions in Sexual Ethics: Moral Theology and the Challenge of AIDS* (London: Chapman, 1998).

92. Curran, *American Catholic Social Ethics*, pp. 26-91.

93. John C. Ford, "Morality of Obliteration Bombing," *Theological Studies* 5 (1944): 261-309.

94. Donald E. Pelotte, *John Courtney Murray: Theologian in Conflict* (New York: Paulist, 1976).

95. Broderick, *Right Reverend New Dealer*, pp. 170-85.

96. Richard P. McBrien, *Caesar's Coin: Religion and Politics in America* (New York: Macmillan, 1987).

97. Pastoral Constitution on the Church in the Modern World, nn. 40-45, in *Vatican Council II*, ed. Flannery, pp. 939-47.

98. National Conference of Catholic Bishops, *The Challenge of Peace: God's Promise and Our Response* (Washington, D.C.: U.S. Catholic Conference, 1983); National Conference of Catholic Bishops, *Economic Justice for All: Pastoral Letter on*

Catholic Social Teaching and the U.S. Economy (Washington, D.C.: U.S. Catholic Conference, 1986).

99. Robert P. Hunt and Kenneth L. Grasso, eds., *John Courtney Murray and the American Civil Conversation* (Grand Rapids, Mich.: Eerdmans, 1992).

100. Charles E. Curran, Margaret A. Farley, and Richard A. McCormick, eds., *Feminist Ethics and the Catholic Moral Tradition: Readings in Moral Theology No. 9* (New York: Paulist, 1996).

101. R. Bruce Douglass and David Hollenbach, eds., *Catholicism and Liberalism: Contributions to American Public Philosophy* (Cambridge: Cambridge University Press, 1994).

102. Ernst Troeltsch, *The Social Teaching of the Christian Churches*, 2 vols. (New York: Harper, 1960), vol. 1, pp. 331-82.

103. Lisa Sowle Cahill, "Feminist Ethics and the Challenge of Cultures," *Proceedings of the Catholic Theological Society of America* 48 (1993): 65-83; Margaret A. Farley, "Feminism and Universal Morality," in *Prospect for a Common Morality*, ed. Gene Outka and John P. Reeder, Jr. (Princeton: Princeton University Press, 1993), pp. 170-90.

THE PÈRE MARQUETTE LECTURES IN THEOLOGY

1969 *The Authority for Authority*
    Quentin Quesnell
      Marquette University

1970 *Mystery and Truth*
    John Macquarrie
      Union Theological Seminary

1971 *Doctrinal Pluralism*
    Bernard Lonergan, S.J.
      Regis College, Ontario

1972 *Infallibility*
    George A. Lindbeck
      Yale University

1973 *Ambiguity in Moral Choice*
    Richard A. McCormick, S.J.
      Bellarmine School of Theology

1974 *Church Membership as a Catholic and Ecumenical Problem*
    Avery Dulles, S.J.
      Woodstock College

1975 *The Contributions of Theology to Medical Ethics*
    James Gustafson
      University of Chicago

1976 *Religious Values in an Age of Violence*
    Rabbi Marc Tannenbaum
      Director of National Interreligious Affairs
      American Jewish Committee, New York City

1977 *Truth Beyond Relativism: Karl Mannheim's Sociology of Knowledge*
Gregory Baum
St. Michael's College

1978 *A Theology of 'Uncreated Energies'*
George A. Maloney, S.J.
John XXIII Center for Eastern Christian Studies
Fordham University

1980 *Method in Theology: An Organon For Our Time*
Frederick E. Crowe, S.J.
Regis College, Toronto

1981 *Catholics in the Promised Land of the Saints*
James Hennesey, S.J.
Boston College

1982 *Whose Experience Counts in Theological Reflection?*
Monika Hellwig
Georgetown University

1983 *The Theology and Setting of Discipleship in the Gospel of Mark*
John R. Donahue, S.J.
Jesuit School of Theology, Berkeley

1984 *Should War be Eliminated? Philosophical and Theological Investigations*
Stanley Hauerwas
Notre Dame University

1985 *From Vision to Legislation: From the Council to a Code of Laws*
Ladislas M. Orsy, S.J.
The Catholic University of America

1986 *Revelation and Violence: A Study in Contextualization*
    Walter Brueggemann
        Eden Theological Seminary
        St. Louis, Missouri

1987 *Nova et Vetera: The Theology of Tradition in American
    Catholicism*
    Gerald Fogarty
        University of Virginia

1988 *The Christian Understanding of Freedom and the History
    of Freedom in the Modern Era: The Meeting and Confron-
    tation Between Christianity and the Modern Era in a
    Postmodern Situation*
    Walter Kasper
        University of Tübingen

1989 *Moral Absolutes: Catholic Tradition, Current Trends, and
    the Truth*
    William F. May
        Catholic University of America

1990 *Is Mark's Gospel a Life of Jesus? The Question of Genre*
    Adela Yarbro Collins
        University of Notre Dame

1991 *Faith, History and Cultures: Stability and Change in
    Church Teachings*
        Walter H. Principe, C.S.B.
        University of Toronto

1992 *Universe and Creed*
    Stanley L. Jaki
        Seton Hall University

1993 *The Resurrection of Jesus Christ: Some Contemporary Issues*
    Gerald G. O'Collins, S.J.
        Gregorian Pontifical University

1994 *Seeking God in Contemporary Culture*
      Most Reverend Rembert G. Weakland, O.S.B.
      Archbishop of Milwaukee

1995 *The Book of Proverbs and Our Search for Wisdom*
      Richard J. Clifford, S.J.
        Weston Jesuit School of Theology

1996 *Orthodox and Catholic Sister Churches: East is West and
      West is East*
      Michael A. Fahey, S.J.
        University of St. Michael's College, Toronto

1997 *'Faith Adoring the Mystery': Reading the Bible with St.
      Ephræm the Syrian*
      Sidney H. Griffith
        Catholic University of America

1998 *Is There Life after Death?*
      Jürgen Moltmann
        Eberhard-Karls Universität
        Tübingen, Germany

1999 *Moral Theology at the End of the Century*
      Charles E. Curran
        Elizabeth Scurlock University Professor of
          Human Values
        Southern Methodist University

About the Père Marquette Lecture Series

The Annual Père Marquette Lecture Series began at Marquette University in the Spring of 1969. Ideal for classroom use, library additions, or private collections, the Père Marquette Lecture Series has received international acceptance by scholars, universities, and libraries. Hardbound in blue cloth with gold stamped covers. Uniform style and price ($15 each). Some reprints with soft covers. Regular reprinting keeps all volumes available. Ordering information (purchase orders, checks, and major credit cards accepted):

Book Masters Distribution Services
1444 U.S. Route 42
P.O. Box 388
Ashland OH 44903

Order Toll-Free (800) 247-6553
fax: (419) 281 6883

Editorial Address:
Dr. Andrew Tallon, Director
Marquette University Press
Box 1881
Milwaukee WI 53201-1881

phone:	(414) 288-7298
fax:	(414) 288-3300
internet:	andrew.tallon@marquette.edu
web:	www.marquette.edu/mupress/

ISBN 0-87462-579-3

9 780874 625790

51500